PAUL

PHOTOGRAPHS BY ANDY CROFTS

THIS DAY IN MUSIC BOOKS
www.thisdayinmusicbooks.com

FOREWORD

Andy Crofts is a very talented man. He's got a great artistic and visual eye, I believe. I've not seen him take a bad shot. Ever! And so to the photos in this book, his first collection, which conjures up dressing rooms, hotels, planes, cars, trains and then......the fantastic shows we've done together over the last ten years (oh yes, ten!!) But even with those feelings aside, I really love his work for its spontaneity, composition, lighting and his imagination.

I hope you do too.

Paul Weller June 2020

A LUCID DREAM

Throughout my life I have always been a dreamer. Head in the clouds I spent many a day looking out of a rainy window lost in my own thoughts with my guitar or camera in hand. As a child I had no idea what this feeling was. To me it just felt like some kind of hunger inside of me that made me see or feel things differently. I was an only child raised by my mother and my grandparents and came from a relatively small family. So I think I generated this need to create purely from being confined to my own imagination.

It was in my teens that I found the spark for photography. I remember seeing a little SLR camera in a second-hand shop and felt compelled to get it. I went through my things and rounded up some bits and bobs to sell and exchange for the camera. About £25, I think. Although it was a cheap camera it was my first and belonged to me. The feeling I got when looking through the lens was unreal. It felt like I could finally see after so many years of being blind. This new vision, which had a depth of field and a new perspective on things, was my awakening and became one of the most natural choices I ever made in my life.

Music and photography have always gone hand in hand for me. The raw expression that both give has led me to this point in my life and through my music I have been in situations that have opened some life-changing doors. And meeting Paul Weller was the most surreal door I ever opened. I have never seen myself as a lucky person in the sense of winning things or being picked for anything in particular, but being asked to join Paul's band in 2008 was the luck I had been waiting all my life for and reignited all creativity in my brain that had been almost crushed through the chores of everyday life.

Since joining the band I have always been waving a camera around and I noticed that slowly and unintentionally over the years I had gathered a collection of photographs that I think now need to be seen. Paul has always been very good with me about my photography and very supportive. I asked him straight up if he minded me taking photos of him and he was great about it. So I saw this as a green light and most boundaries had been lifted, giving me access to most things whilst being respectful at the same time.

My photographs are never planned. They are always instant and usually come from us passing somewhere that catches my eye. I think Paul trusts me enough with my camera now to understand how I may see things, and these opportunities usually just appear out of nowhere. I often say, 'Paul, hold it there a second,' and I'll quickly take a snap or two of him before we continue. I see all my photographs purely as me just observing moments. That's about as posed as we ever get. I also very rarely crop my pictures, as I believe the whole image is the truth. Some photographers take many pics and select the best part of the frame, which is great if that's their style, but for me I like to take it as I see the final image.

This book is a series of observations from over the years of travelling and being part of the Paul Weller band. I wanted to keep the photographs mostly random, without them being chronologically placed throughout. I think this gives you more of a feeling of the variety of situations we encounter. I've never seen myself as a professional, just somebody who feels the moment and has to catch it in some artistic form, whether that be in photography or songwriting. I'm eternally grateful for being chosen as part of the band and given the freedom to be as creative as I please, and this feeds the constant hunger in me.

I love Paul like a brother, and I'm honoured to see him work up close, as I do. He's an artist who continues to inspire, with no boundaries in his music and creations. I'm proud to be part of it all and even more proud that he trusts me to capture some of it with my eyes.

Enjoy – Andy Crofts

Love
Rock
Ellisons

Lost Souls

One of the wonderful things about travelling and touring is that I get to roam on my days off. Whilst making my ONE documentary I had one of my influential moments in Amsterdam, where I walked for miles with my camera soaking in my surroundings and I felt so connected. These feelings are everything to me and feed me like the greenest apple! Another place that does this for me is New York. I Love NYC! I love its energy, rawness and grit. I guess its very similar to London in that way and I feel I could point my camera anywhere and get a good picture.

Blackstar

Back Seat View

We once played a festival in San Francisco called "Strictly Bluegrass fest" and judging by the title it didn't seem like the right match for our music BUT... how wrong I was. The show was amazing and the crowd were just beautiful. This was back in 2015 when I played the keys before moving onto bass guitar, so I took advantage of a gap between some chords and got this picture. Apart from sounding heavenly, a hammond organ acts as a great table top for resting cameras on.

HSB
Paul Weller

SOYMILK
SOYMILK

On Sunset

I love this picture. I remembe we were all hanging out backstage and there was this beautiful sunset creeping through the window. A kind of holy sunset that swallows the whole room for a fleeting moment. In the split second that this photograph was taken, I wonder what Paul was thinking. Was he thinking at all or just free of thought lost in the sunset?

A KIND
REVOLUTION
PAUL WELLER
LATE SHOW

On the road

I have always loved the tour bus. When we are away for a long time it becomes our second home and considering its limited space, we all somehow manage to find our little areas. I do so much thinking on the bus. I have written songs, poetry, filmed and taken photos of every cloud you can imagine. I love our touring family. Its our second home.

THE LIBERTINES
Peaches
GALACTIC
WILCO
2004
THE FILLMORE
GUIDED BY VOICES
THE FILLMORE
MINISTRY
GOMEZ

IM WHERE I SHOULD BE
LONG TIME
IN THE CROWD
WHITE SKY
CORNERSHOP
PAPER CHASE
SATURNS PATTERN
GOING MY WAY
STARLITE
MOODS
EVER HAD IT BLUE
INTO TOMORROW
PICK IT UP
SUZIES ROOM
FRIDAY ST
PORCELAIN GODS
CLOUDS
PEACOCK SUIT
START!
SINKING
CITY STREETS
LONG HOT SUMMER
CHANGINGMAN
MALICE

Selfies on iPhone X

Inner Light

I can't remember where this was taken but I think it was Italy. It was a really hot day and we found this nice little roof terrace backstage to hang out on. There were buildings surrounding the area but somehow the sunlight was reflecting on to the buildings windows. A very surreal glow was projected onto the terrace and against the wall where Paul was standing. I don't think one other person even noticed but I just kept quiet and clicked away. It was perfect and almost like gods natural studio lighting.

A KIND
REVOL
WELLER

KYO-ICHI

faces ☺

Sometimes I like to take my camera on stage at the end of a show as it's amazing to look back at all the people's faces. For every face there is a different story. Each person has different connections to the songs which have created a spectrum of memories across the crowd. All the love in the room can be captured effortlessly in one single click ♥

LIQUOR
plcu.com
Easy breezy
Auto loans

I left my heart in San francisco

One of my most inspired times was walking the streets of San fran. We had a day off and I just picked up my camera and headphones and walked and walked. I'm not one of these people who walk religiously but I just couldnt stop. I loved every minute of it feeling like I was in a Woody Allen film like Play it again Sam or Steve McQueens Bullitt. This taxi shot was actually early in the morning of the day we had to leave. I didnt have time to walk the distance again so I jumped a cab.

NO
PARKING
ANY
TIME

Ed Sullivan Theatre

A very special moment for me "US" was playing the Ed Sullivan theatre in New York as part of The Late Show. We are all familiar with all the greats who have graced that stage and have watched The Beatles footage endless times so it meant a lot for us to be there and was a stand out for me.
The main room was much smaller than I imagined as we are all used to watching them old TV shows where everything looks bigger. One thing that caught my eye was these old theatre/cinema style chairs in deep red velvet. They looked like originals. So on that day Paul was wearing a cool Op Art top with his hexagonal glasses so I just knew the black and white against the red was gonna look perfect. CLASSIC!

EXIT
EXIT

MTA
SERIES 980

BROOKS
CAFÉ
DANIEL'S
Condomania

Reflections

This is my favourite photograph from when we once stayed in Glasgow. As I stood outside I had to ask Paul to just hold it there a second as the moment was just perfect. It's as if the clouds and the trees in the reflection are projections of my imagination onto the glass. I really am happy with this picture.

GB

GB

PAUL WELLER

A KIND
REVOL
UTION
PAUL WELLER

"Ringo"

When I'm walking around with my camera I love to see stickers and signs on lamp posts and walls. I find myself snapping away all the time. I found this one interesting though. A lost Beatle! Ringo! I hope he was actually found but this was in central New York so who knows.

SOZE
NYCX • PPP
LOST DOG - REWARD
"Ringo"
Red-ish Brown Retriever/Ridgeback Mix
Approx 75 lbs, Very friendly
Ringo was tied up in front of Fresh Food Deli and Grocery on West Broadway just south of Canal on the evening of Wednesday Aug 20/early morning August 21
Family heartbroken, please call with any info.
917-208-0473/917-833-8859
REWARD

CRANBERRY

Marshall

MEMOTRON
Blackstar
Blackstar
Marshall

Menlove Avenue.

I can't explain the amount of times I have visited John Lennon's old Mendips home. Being huge Beatle fans it's almost like a religious thing that whenever we pass anything related we have to stop. The whole Beatle thing still fascinates us, well me and Paul. I think the thing we talk about the most is The Beatles...and why not!

The other side of the Changing man

Pauls sense of humour is brilliant. When all the boys are together we are always laughing around. We all have very similar taste so it makes our little gang more unbreakable. As we all know, Paul is an icon and a real english treasure aswell as being one of the naturally cool people I have ever met. So when you see his other side which is very funny it really lights up a room when he walks in. I guess we all expect our idols to be superhuman but we also expect them to be human too.

NAMBA
ORIENTAL
HOTEL
BREZEL
ROLL
ドリンク
セット
+¥100
ブレッツェルロール

N WABASH AV
44 E

Thick as Thieves

Kenny Wheeler has been part of the Weller family for a long time now. Since way back in The Jam days and after knowing him some time now I have always admired his dedication and commitment to Paul. I love this photograph as it reminds me of a couple of kids messing about on a School trip.

KEXP
90.3 FM
SEATTLE
KEXP.ORG

Natural Balance

Finding a balance with my music and photography on the road can sometimes be difficult as literally can not be everywhere at once so I have to choose my moments perfectly. These moments are usually on a whim and of the moment. Soundchecks are always a good time for me to catch Paul playing.

ONE WAY

Blackstar
Blackstar

放置自転車
禁止区域

English Rose

During our rehearsals for the Other Aspects show at the Royal Festival Hall London we were joined by the lovely Lucy Rose who has the most beautiful voice. Paul has always been great at championing other artists and featuring special guests at his shows.

8
13
13

Invisibility

I love these moments of the mind thinking. Sometimes I'm just sat in front or in the same room as Paul and I have to know when it's right to use my camera. Invisibility is something that comes with trust and it would be impossible to capture these intimate moments without it.

POMONA
KCRW &
GOLDENVOICE
PAUL WELLER
TONIGHT!
POMONA
KCRW &
PAUL WELLER
TONIGHT!

MILES
DAVIS
COMPLETE
LIVE AT
PLUGGED
NICKEL
1965

Love by the Jukebox Light

Many have seen it but it really is a thing of beauty. I think there was only ever a handful made but its amazing. I once saw another one at the old GO Discs offices back in the day. Paul has a great selection of some of his favourite songs in there. Sounds great and looks amazing!

A KIND REVOLUTION
PAUL WELLER
You've Got It Bad
PAUL WELLER
PAUL WELLER
STANLEY ROAD

Looking Glass

I have always been drawn to mirrors and shadows in my photography... I like reflections. I love silhouettes. A mirror is like a glimpse into another dimension, an alter ego, a parallel universe..... The truth!

BARBICAN

Store

Manhattan

swissport

Mobile Phone Photography

Like most people, one thing I have on me most of the time is a phone. I'm not really a fan of phone photography but you can get a pretty instant picture. I'm sometime too busy to get to my big camera so I have to use my phone. After looking through them all I realised I had a nice collection and decided to add them to the book. I guess a photo is a photo however you take it.

ROCK VINYL
VINTAGE '60s & '70s
ROCK VINYL
WE FILE "LIBRARY STYLE" BY ARTIST LAST NAME

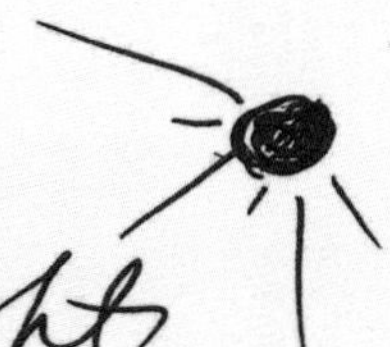

Painting with Light

I feel compelled to take photographs.
I feel I have to and do not really have choice.
I am fascinated that we can capture a moment
and save it for a lifetime. I will always be amazed.
True time travel...

A KIND
REVOL
UTION
PAUL WELLER
Marshall
Marshall
A KIND
REVOL
UTION
PAUL WELLER

I never read,
I just look
at pictures.
Andy Warhol
10/2–17/3 1968

POST NO BILLS
POST BILLS
POST PROTEST POEMS
streetings
POST
PROTEST
POEMS

ALIMENTARI
MOLTENI

ALIMENTARI
MOLTENI

OLD TOWN
ST LAWRENCE MARKET NEIGHBOURHOOD
OFFICE
JOE FRESH

KATSCHIGARE
loch jetzt albern.
POLICE
ABER
HALLO
VENUES
PADDY
RATS
I AM NOAH
E.J.
SHANNON
Mammoth
grinder
BLIND BASTARDS
NO HOPE
WIGHT
GET RICH
OR TRY
SHARING...

Truck Stop Blues

There is a lot of driving for us in america so naturally we stop all over the place for food etc. This photo was taken early in the morning after a very long drive across the states. Im not sure where this was but it was the classic american truck stop breakfast all sat up against the bar.

GIVE $3
GET $12

BBC
RADIO
2
Piano

ASTRA
ASTRA

Aspects

This picture is during Paul's actual vocal take for the song Aspects. I'm so lucky that he lets me float about when he's doing these things. I am always aware if I'm in the way but I try to move with the room. Sometimes a phone photo has an innocence that others can't catch.

Fender

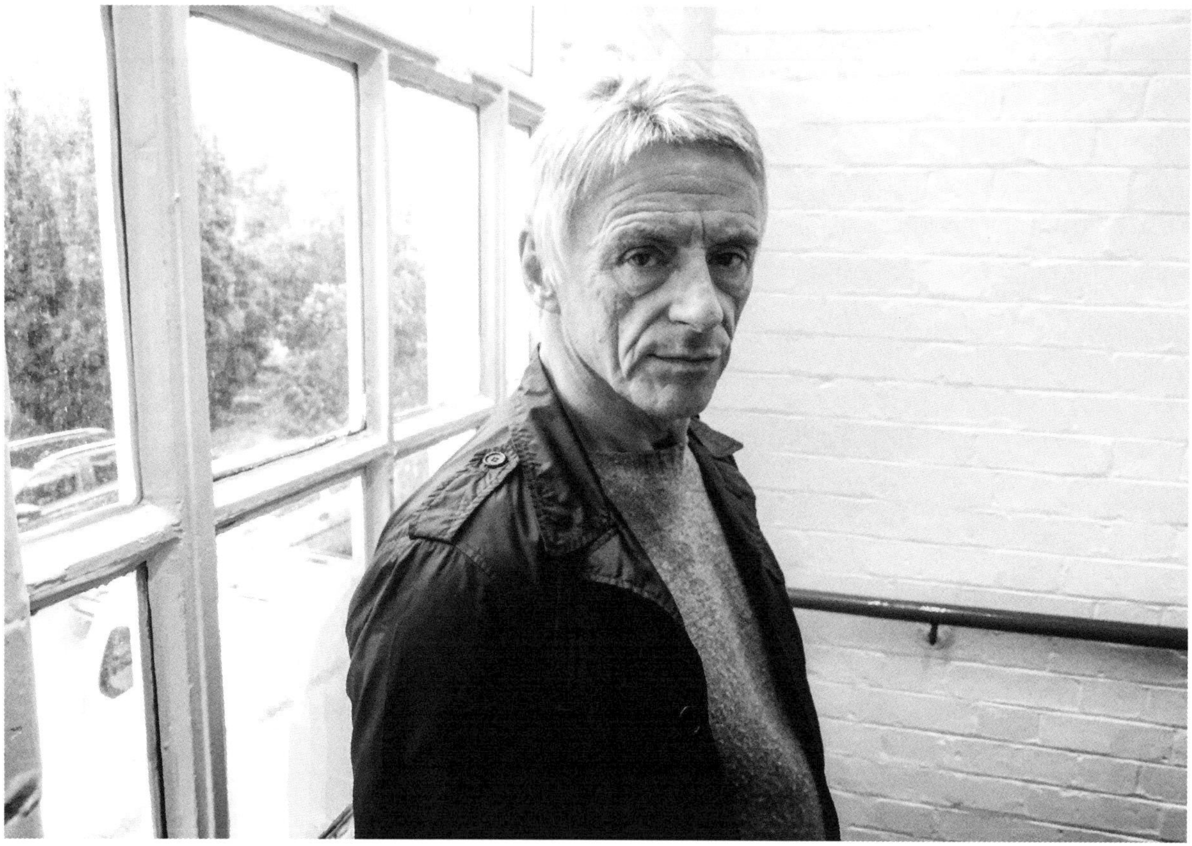

WiFi
STAGE
BÜHNE
FRONT
of
HOUSE

Molteni

I love it when we get to a venue and there is interesting things around. This photograph was just by the back entrance to the venue (somewhere in europe). It was just perfect and real nice graffiti. Pauls t-shirt against the wall colours was a perfect fit. Once again with natural light. I very rarely use a flash etc as natural light gives the real deal for me.

ALIMENTARI
MOLTENI

STAGE DOOR

7:30pm:
DOORS
10:45pm:
Curfew

Marshall

HOT PRESS

Weller
GUILD

SDR
CULTURE
CS
STUDIO

Equanimity

In a world so divided by love, hate, power and colour,
I feel blessed to be around inspiring people.

People who create
People who Love
People who share
People who trust

These photographs of Paul capture the natural aura and energy that one positive soul can bring to the world. So I hope that just for one minute, you can find some escape in this book and some soulful inspiration.

Thank you to Paul for allowing me to observe part of his life through a lens. Allowing me the freedom and trust to create and feed my imagination. Allowing me to be part of the music and the adventures. I am truly blessed. Andy X

A catalogue record for this book is available from the British Library.

ISBN 978-1-8380783-3-1

Thanks to Gary Bishop who worked with Andy on the design, Dave Evely from Sound Performance for production ideas and Richard Bowes for helping bring this project to the table. Band photo in Sydney Australia by Mark Carr. A huge thank you to Claire Moon for her support and encouragement. Foreword photograph of Paul & Andy by Hannah Weller.
www.andycrofts.com www.paulweller.com

Production Liz Sánchez and Neil Cossar

Printed in the UK by Sound Performance

This Day In Music Books Bishopswood Road, Prestatyn, LL19 9PL

THIS DAY IN MUSIC BOOKS

www.thisdayinmusicbooks.com

Email: editor@thisdayinmusic.com

Exclusive Distributors: Music Sales Limited 14/15 Berners St London W1T 3JL